THEATER, STORIES AND SCENES OF FORGOTTEN PEOPLE (SECOND EDITION) CORRECTED AND EXPANDED

The prophecies of the times open the understanding:

If you found this world built, why should you sacrifice it?

Decadence, Imperialism, and ambition, lead to destruction; what is the use of globalization, when there are obstruction borders?

The culture justice is not only what happens also, why happen and who make the happen.

After darkness shines the light.

I feel freedom at a liberty world, really I never has been catching up my dream illusion.

The liberty is not only to preach, is to practice.

CONTENTS

WEIGHTING THE FIRST EDITION..................1
PRESENTATION..................3
EXPRESSION OF THE AUTHOR..................5
PROLOGUE..................6
PRESENTATION TO THE NEW EDITION..................9

PART I: Short Stories

Nostalgia for the Devil..................13
The Sad Man of the Arrabal..................26
The Globe's Forgotten Ones..................38
Sealed Pact..................46
Violence at the School..................54

PART II: Theater

The Lackey's Deceit (monologue)..................60
The Rite of Rebellion..................75
The Trial of a Corrupt and Unjust Man..................111

WEIGHTING THE FIRST EDITION

What kind of motivation can a young man have to invest his leisure time in questions that, even if very literary, are too serious? It is no easy to answer that question just at a time when an important part of youth is torn between the duty quasi–obligated multiple task s oriented to subsistence or pure fun.

However, at the same time, what prompts this young man to venture into genres other than literary expression, such as theater and story?

Mariano Morillo B., a Social communicator and an eternal lover of theater and life, is not so youth in these things despite his physical youth.

It is recognized, to the Mariano, intense participation in the Dominican cultural life, and particularly, in the Autonomous University of Santo Domingo (UASD).

Also, parallel, a constant search for expression, a permanent questioning about its environment, about what there is and what there is not. Grounder of daily life, search of multiple message that express it, liked proverbs and "saying" of popular sentences, Mariano Morillo B. would seem to extrapolate that search to the literary imagination, where the social retains a significant motivation, while it manifests itself as a particular concern for fate, but not for the sake of it, but for the community's destiny.

The stories that appear in this work, as well as the theatrical approaches, reflect serenely much of the cosmos that intrigues its young author.

Profesor: Onofre de la Rosa.

PRESENTATION:

This presentation of this second edition on English, Corresponds to the first edition in Spanish published by the autonomous University of Santo Domingo (UASD) during the dean of Dr. Luciano Castillo in the faculty of Humanities, who referred to the author in the following terms:

Mariano Morillo B. recently published an essay on universal theater.

Now dares to venture into the theme of stories and plays and publish them.

We have used the verb "dare," on purpose because the young Mariano Morillo B. he has determined to do something difficult and Risky when penetrating such delicate literary genres.

It is rare in our days to find a young who dedicates himself to socio-cultural tasks that seem no to interest contemporary youth, and that when he dedicates himself to enter the literary aspects in our environment, he inclines towards the easiest thing to deal with.

In this book, Mariano Morillo B. do what many young people disdain, introducing themselves to the storyteller and in the theater, very difficult and delicate aspects in their handling and treatment in the literature.

Its content is as follows:

The first part consists of five stories and the second part brings us three plays.

Each reader will judge for himself the quality of the work that

Mariano Morillo B. offers us on this occasion, so we will refrain from issuing any value judgment on them, to not positively or negatively influence him.

Now, we are of the opinion that young people like Mariano Morillo., must be encouraged and encouraged to continue creating and researching and publish the results of these activities, which will greatly benefit our society.

With these brief words, we want to present the writings of Mariano Morillo B.

Dr. Luciano Castillo.

EXPRESSION OF THE AUTHOR

After reading the weighting of the first edition of this work, it should be noted that a few years after the publication made by the autonomous University of Santo Domingo, UASD, in the – Literature and society N9 collection, was corrected and expanded, at the time the English edition was processed, that is why the readers who came to acquire the first edition, when reading this one again, will realized that other titles have been added such as the story " Violence in the School", and the theatrical satire " Judgment to an Unjust Corrupted", both written in the United States, and published in the English edition.

So understanding that readings seriously hurt ignorance, I urge you to enjoy this reading.

Thank you.

FOREWORD

These texts represent the beginning of a career in literature and theater.

The author Mariano Morillo B.; in this collection, he fixes his restless gaze, his intellect, and human sensibility, on those situations common to the great rainbow of the Latin American peoples, and to all the marginalized peoples of the world.

As he states, they are not "sophisticated" it is not his intention.

Mariano Morillo B. aims to create awareness vehicles that provide positive thoughts to an audience that has been deprived of Quality Theater and literature due to lack of education, the negative influence of the media, or the simple lack of resources.

Of course, Mariano Morillo is very experienced and will not leave aside the spectacular and passionate element that runs through our veins.

That last one catches my attention because in the theater plays Mariano resorts to the structure and theme of the sacramental cars, a kind of religious procession organized by the craft guilds in the European Middle Ages.

This still serves as a model for many artists and groups throughout the Latin American continent, both in the traditional and in contemporary.

Perhaps the use of spectacular elements, along with themes and characters are drawn " brush fat", are the most effective shields for those who want to criticize without being specific.

I also imagine that the format would be effective for public health campaigns in remote or marginalized areas, in the city or the countryside, and I am sure that the author would be delighted with the idea.

These are the words, then, of Mariano.

Mariano Morillo is a fighter for culture, an awakened being, and his talent and heart bring his work of great satisfaction.

I like to join my efforts as a translator, who also aspire to the simplicity that one of the great masters advised me, Mariano, and give a contribution to the great tradition of Latin American popular theater.

Walter Krochmal.

PRESENTATION TO THE NEW EDITION

With high and great consideration, I praise the people who have insisted on pointing out from the heart, our concern for social problems.

It is true, although in dialectics nothing remains static in time, that concern was, has been and will continue to be, and it can be said that those people who in my beginnings sat those expressions of futuristic prophecies, without a doubt, traced the guidelines that encouraged me to move forward.

This New edition of "Theater Stories And Scenes of a forgotten People" that appeared for the first time, in the American market, in English, so it has also been selling in England and other English speaking countries, with great success, it is for me, pleasantly satisfying, to deliver it again to the English-speaking readers, in order to evaluate the conditions under which time cements the essence and the form.

For this new edition in English the extension of the were inserted so that the story " violence in the school" can be read, and the play "The Trial Of a Corrupt and unjust Man, which has been staged with great success, in the New York stages.

As in the first edition, we tried to take into account those five difficulties for those who write the truth, which Bertolt Brecht stated with great clarity that: "anyone who tries to fight lies and ignorance and write the truth, must have the courage and sagacity to recognize it, the art of making it manageable as a weapon, the judgment of choosing those in whose hands it would be more effective, and the skill of propagating it among them".

Value has not been lacking, I am a communicator, the communicator is a server; if you are a communicator you have to commit to society, and I recognize the essence of its problems.

In this edition, the first part of this work includes five stories inspired by the idiosyncrasy of the people of the world's inhabitants who live in marginalized sectors or in rural areas that have not been developed by government sectors or high economic power.

The second part is composed of two plays and a monologue; here, historical experiences of social injustices are reproduced.

PART ONE:
Short Stories

Nostalgia for the Devil

The Sad Man of the Arrabal

The Globe's Forgotten Ones

Sealed Pact

Violence at the School

Nostalgia for the Devil

He had finished loading the purchase into the last customer's car and was waiting for him to pull out. It was a day like another day, except that it was 18 July, and the rain would occasionally surprise the sun, forcing it to hide.

Homero had been working in that food warehouse for a while, and though he was not over the hill, he had turned forty a month earlier. The day started to vanish. He felt defeated inside; he looked guilty, but it was just his being "run down," feeling like he had been put through a mill.

It was the start of the third week in July. He was waiting for the first opportunity to ask Don Pedro, the warehouse owner, to give his son Jacinto a job sweeping.

For a moment, Don Pedro did not think it was appropriate, but he realized that Homero had been working for him for twelve years. He told him to bring Jacinto in on Monday, out of consideration. Homero felt fortunate, and happiness coursed through his veins:

"Thank God and thank you, my son's going to work."

Don Pedro saw the joy in his face and reaffirming his promise, added:

"He'll have a job starting Monday. I want him to produce."

"Don't worry about that, Don Pedro, Jacinto works when there's work to be done," Homero added enthusiastically.

Don Pedro, with the rich man's guile, made it clear:

"It's not for nothing, but you saw me fire that woman for being a softie."

"This warehouse is filthy!" he said, giving the floor inside an inspection.

Don Pedro had counted the till and they closed everything: He offered to walk Homero home since he was going to the place nearby where he had commissioned a welder to make a door for the warehouse.

Homero was thinking that Saturday, with the money he made, he would be able to pay his compadre the twenty pesos he owed him, and the other twenty out of the forty he made would be spent at home.

The next day was Sunday, and the crowds were everywhere. Jacinto was sitting in front of his house in a chair propped against a wall, chatting with two friends who were digging a hole for a latrine that was under construction. He never imagined that the turbulent atmosphere was because of the goons scouring the neighborhood for its young men. They thought that Sunday the lottery peddlers would do a lot of business. They were thinking this until a patrol officer drove up, and without paying attention to the place, came out of the vehicle. The sergeant demanded of him:

"Let's go, get in," he said with a certain sarcasm and the pride his uniform made him feel. Jacinto, who still could not understand or believe what, was happening to his friends and him, asked, and surprised:

"Why, sergeant?"

The sergeant, giving him to explanation, believing himself and Indian chief along with two assistant officers, shove them into the patrol car, where they fell on top of each other.

Homero was not home. He had gone out earlier that they.

Lucrecia his wife was coming back from the street and her usual lottery game. Her idea was to set up a little candy store if one of her numbers won the jackpot. Her illusions vanished when a patrol car crammed with people spattered her with mud as it drove by; she realized that they had Jacinto with them.

"Hey! Where are you taking my son?" She asked the sergeant, whose dentures almost fell out as he replied:

"He's going for a spin with us, old lady!"

The detainees were so uncomfortable; any average religious little old woman would have thought it as a sacrilege.

Lucrecia was very perplexed.

A moment later more patrol units appeared: the detainees were so many that eight units needed to transport them.

Jacinto was a young nineteen years old. He had never been in jail, even for a social visit. He was a young man who "gave nothing, but took away nothing."

To tell the truth, no one knew the reasons for those detentions, but the cause was a complaint lodged by the lieutenant's mother-in-law, a hunchback woman who looked like a camel in the Sahara when she walked; she had a house in the neighborhood where Homero, Jacinto's father, lived with his family. Doña Plauda, which is what her son-in-law called her, stated that Saturday night she left a cow that produced milk for her grandson, the lieutenant's son, at home; that ; she'd left it under lock and key, because of the thunder and lightning, and she was afraid that the cow might get wet and catch a cold; that she'd left it unguarded because she'd tried to locate one of the men who worked for her son-in-law and hadn't been successful, but this man's absence had made her son-in-law lock him up for five days, and thinking that people in that neighborhood were decent, she trusted her cow to the untested custom of the neighborhood, and the next day when she went to look for it so another subordinate could milk it, she found nothing; they'd taken the cow and "cleaned out the house" so the lieutenant ordered all the detentions, because he understood that the people in the neighborhood were fools. That afternoon, the detachment he was assigned to have so many visitors that were allowed to stray. The lieutenant's voice rang out, deep and aggressive, like an unruly dog's bark.

"Wait over there: Only one person for each detainee can talk to me"

That afternoon the lieutenant felt like a detective about to question the lowlifes, as he called them, whom he had detained. The issue was property damage, damage to his mother-in-law and above all to his means for feeding his son; he had more than enough reason to think of "the detained as little things that don't matter."

Homero was indignant when he saw his wife:

"What's the matter, Lucrecia?"

Lucrecia, with some nostalgia, related that morning's story briefly:

"They took Jacinto prisoner and his friends who came to dig the latrine hole."

Homero bit his lips, and said to himself, now maybe I will lose my chance at a job.

"Nothing happened that second, but Homero felt as if he were watching his naked mother showing off to an audience that was booing her.

Without a second's delay, they went to take Jacinto some food. When they got there, they found things were quieter, people had come to order; the agent on patrol outside the precinct was getting ready to interrogate them.

Homero, without beating around the bush, started to explain what was happening, when all of a sudden, the lieutenant intervened:

"One of you two come with me, the other stays here.

They won't be able to see him anyway."

"No, lieutenant, my wife is interested in what you might be able to tell us about the boys," said Homero, feeling ill at ease.

The official was confused for a second, but sprang back:

"Who are you to make that kind of bald-faced statement here: what do you want?"

Lucrecia, knowing that Homero might answer in the wrong tone of voice, stepped forward:

"They detained our son Jacinto, and this food's for him: we want to know why he's here."

The lieutenant grabbed the food with his bony hands, tapped the containers, and passed them to the sergeant with eyes like an owl in sunlight; he would not take his sights off his chest, said:

"That so-called Jacinto has a toothache."

Homero, hearing this, said:

"Lieutenant, you're telling me my boy has a toothache; let us see him."

The official, rubbing his badge, replied:

"That fellow's here for an investigation. You can't see him." Lucrecia, who was following the conversation closely, begged him with her deep-set eyes:

"If we can't see him, I want to send him these fifty cents, and I want you…"

The lieutenant proved greedy; he tore, the fifty cents, from

Lucrecia hand, and again charged the sergeant, who had returned by this time, to give them over.

The sergeant, who was the lieutenant's senior, was annoyed; when he returned he looked like an angry chimpanzee.

One of the women visitors yelled, at him from the outside:

"Hey, loco!"

The sergeant kept his silence, unshakeable.

The woman, who was used to getting agitated, added:

"When you' are in your headquarters, you don't pay attention to anybody.

The lieutenant asked her to dust the desk, and the sergeant thought to himself: you can't escape these damn whores, and the lieutenant's trying to make a fool of me.

Homero bit his lips silently. He had been a soldier, but not a police officer; still, he never thought that a veteran would be treated as if the lieutenant was treating him. He told himself that from now on everything would change.

What made him truly bitter was when the lieutenant asked him to go outside and stop making a nuisance of himself. It felt like a blow, and he answered like a wounded animal.

"Sir: don't fart so high in the air. People with higher ranks than you have been skinned; the only difference between us, which is what makes you a man, is that you wear a uniform and carry a weapon...

The lieutenant wiped off his chest; a rasp choked his throat. Homero had slammed the door in his face; he would hurt his pride. He tried to hold back, but something drove him to get it off his chest: "Shut up, carajo, coño…that's all I need, for you to come and insult me; get out of here and stop talking nonsense if you don't want me to lock you up."

The lieutenant had tried to intimidate him but realized that men like Homero were not a dime a dozen.

Lucrecia, who had stayed quiet as they spoke, broke her silence:

"We're leaving, but I don't want you to lay a hand on my son. If you hit him, you'll have to kill me."

When she finished she caught herself talking alone:

The lieutenant had gone into one of the rooms. The guard kept silent and the sergeant too.

Those who were listening to the conversation had gathered around each other tightly.

Lucrecia took Homero way by the arm and they made their way through the onlookers who were blocking the doorway.

The official came out again, screaming furiously:

"Clear the doorway if you don't want me to lock you all up."

Homero was so discombobulated he thought:

After all, the police are the police, unless someone says something different.

Homero's show made news; it was reported that a brave man had put the lieutenant in his place.

Along the way, someone greeted him:

"Good-bye, don Homero, I heard you made a dessert out of the lieutenant."

Another added:

"He's a devil! He told the truth and didn't stammer!"

Homero replied with a nod and kept on quietly. As they walked he thought about how Don Pedro, the owner of the warehouse, might be able to do something for Jacinto, Don Pedro was not really a millionaire, but he was not too far away from a half million.

That night, when he managed to get to sleep, he dreamt that s boss had to beg for forgiveness, the guilty lieutenant groveled on the floor, and from his alligator-likee position, promised that from now on the innocent would not be pulled out of their houses to help make up a story. The dogs barking interrupted his hollow fantasy.

When he woke up, he thought the dogs were barking because they were hungry and that maybe the devil had made him dream so he would catch a winning lottery number, and once he was rich, there would not be a lieutenant around who would think he was talking nonsense.

Lucrecia interrupted the rhythm of his ideas; she had dreamt that Jacinto died.

"The means long life." --- Replied Homero.
The dogs stopped barking.

The Sad Man of the Arrabal

It was so, once upon a time,
I say: what has always been,
What they say has not been,
What they say has not been,
What will cease to be?

The slum awoke from its deep and slothful lethargy after the satin-feathered rooster, pedaling his wings in the air, left his tree. Everyone knew that the bird's tuneful crowing announced another day; surviving got harder with each dawn, so many came to hate the light of day, and even went for months as enemies of the sun. Robinson Rubio was one of them. Wrapping himself in the blanket and twisting around before he sat up in the edge of the bed, he put his feet on the ground and, shaking his wife, said:

"Get up, Tomasa, it's dawn already."

"Don't pester me," she said, opening her eyes and stretching."

"Woman of God, get up I say, the poor can't sleep so much."

Tomasa, curling up again, begged him:

"Don't be like that, let me sleep a little bit more," and she closed her eyes again.

The main features of the house were the humble condition of people who have no money, and the gas lamp, which you could see through the threshold on a table.

Robinson, vertigo in his brain, grabbed his wife by the legs, pulled her, and forced her to imitate him.

"Carajo, what are you hoping for? If you didn't sleep between last night and now, you're not going to sleep," he said.

Tomasa silently obeyed and faced the fact of the day.

Her first discovery was the prank her son, Tomasito, had pulled: Urinating on her ribs.

She cornered him indignantly: "Shitass kid you peed on yourself while you were awake."

She took him by the underarms and set him on the packed earth floor, which made the boy wail louder until it filled the whole place. Robinson took him in his arms, and to comfort him for his woes, stroked him and said:

"Don't cry, Papi, I'm going to go get you some bread."

Besides, once more, as so many times before, the boy felt some hope in his life and quieted down his bawling until there was a brief silence, which Tomasa broke in desperation, killing her infant's illusions.

"You offer him bread, and I'm the one who gets left with the problem when you go out there," She said with a melancholy air.

Robinson felt a meaty aftertaste in his mouth. He took the boy off himself, and gulped, exclaiming:

"Coño! How I'd like to go to bed one of these nights and not wake up the following day."

Tomasito got scared and wrapped himself securely around one of his father's knees.

"Papi," he uttered, slurring the words.

Robinson looked at his son and stroked his head.

"I'm going out, pawn the red pants," he said to his wife.

Tomasa, her hair hard and uncombed, muttered:

"Son, it's all you have to go out with and you're going to"…

"If we don't do that, what the hell's to eat tonight?" He answered, gruffly.

That's pauper's environment that made him wicked. His wife did not respond. They looked at each other again, and Robinson Rubio left, deep in thought, sad.

Dawn gave way to the sun, whose rays began to decorate the slum. From one house to the next, the almost igneous clarity of the king of planets crept through the cracks.

Robinson left the neighborhood occasionally, his face drawn with sadness. It had been two years since he had been canceled from his position with the Sanitation Department in a state agency, and from then on, he had blamed himself for the dogs he killed over the six years the job lasted.

Cojollo, what fool I was, he told himself, now I realized that those poor dogs turn garbage cans over because they're Hungry. Besides, he thought further: If I did not have to worry about food for anyone, maybe I would be happy.

He was gloomy. He was so possessed that he didn't hear his compadre Joaquin, who called as he ran from behind to catch up to him; only when he felt a slap on his shoulder did he start at his presence.

"Compa Robinson, what are you thinking about?" Asked Joaquin as he gulped for air.

"Oh, compadre, is that you? " Robinson was surprised.

"I was going over there just now," Joaquin said.

They agreed to visit Rogelio, the cobbler, who could solve a small problem for Joaquin.

That Monday began turning into a scorcher, and the residual dirt was becoming a soiled, sticky crust that kept him from moving smoothly. When they arrived, they found Rogelio hugging the taste of alcohol.

From another corner, Rogelio got up, stumbling:

"I …believe …I know you …you seem like my friends."

He grabbed the bottle and asked him to keep him company; yet instead of sharing it with him, they tried to pull him out of his state of alienation.

"Don't you recognize us?" Robinson asked serenely.

"Yes, of course. You look like a shipwrecked sailor to me, Crusoe."

Joaquin stroked the beard-growing all over his face, tapped Robinso's right shoulder. They agreed to leave when Rogelio's wife burst into the bedroom and refused to talk to them; when she saw they were far away, she said to her husband:

"You did well to ignore them."

Rogelio still reeling stroked his wife's face:

"Don't be like that, mi Vida," he said.

"What life, what life," she replied indignantly.

She removed the record and turned off the phonograph. She grabbed Rogelio by the arm, showed him to bed, and there was a silence…

The days flew by desperately, and with them Robinson Rubio's restlessness. Thursday came and was gray and he thought that the temperature might be favorable to face his daily routine; first to a gambling den two blocks from his house, and since he didn't like the drawn-out rhythm of an argument between the rake-off and two players, he kept going. As he walked, he thought about everything: His job, which he needed so badly, and the government that had come into power and bumped him out of it. He also thought about his friends. Did I say his friends?

Oh yes, he had no more chances left to resort to them.

He really had no resources left to exhaust. Since the previous summer he had started going out early and talking to the first person he met; he told them his situation and finally, said that if they had anything to offer, it would be taken.

Now he was at the door to a product export company; he stepped inside where a secretary greeted him."

"Good morning," she said quietly. Nevertheless, her voice was lost in the roar of a trailer truck running its motor, taking the place over.

"What did you say?" the secretary inquired curiously.

"May I see Don Mario?"

"Possibly. What would you like?"

"Tell him that Robinson Rubio wants to see him."

Before announcing the visitor, the young secretary studied him, and then went in a doorway with a sign that said "Administrator."

Robinson was in the waiting room and still had not changed his expression when the secretary returned.

"He says he doesn't know you."

In no hurry at all, he rubbed his hands through his hair extremely slowly and said:

"But we were like brothers; tell him it's his cousin."

"He can't see you…I'm sorry."

Robinson insisted, but it was no use. A brief silence came over the chamber. He looked through the windows and saw the rooftops, the black clouds crisscrossing each other; he spun around out of control to face the door.

"Well, what can we do," he said drily.

The secretary saw the unexpected disappointment in his eyes and shared his desperation for a moment.

"I'm sorry, "she said again.

Robinson understood, he pulled the glass door open and went out into the street. His body was like lead, his feet refused to obey, he felt hollow inside and his eyes filled with tears; he didn't hide it until he discovered workers and students shouting out slogans for givebacks.

It struck him as almost odd, but no, everything was contained in its pain. He could not understand the sudden presence of anti-riot units, who moved in a wedge formation and scattered the ralliers. Some escaped in the nick of time, others faced off with them, some were detained, everything happened at one moment or another; the gases took over the air as the residents closed their doors and ran with their children in their arms.

The day was getting foggy: A group of curious bystanders was staring at a pool of blood on the asphalt.

"Poor man, he looked like good people!" Said one.

"What happened?" Asked another who arrived now.

"That man jumped on top of the car."

"Why? " Asked one with a flattened nose.

"Supposedly he had eight children, he owed a lot at the local store, and they refused to give him credit," said a quarrelsome little fat fellow.

Robinson did not say a thing. He rubbed his eyes, which unfortunately were tearing.

Why? He wondered…

The problem was that his eyes were gazing on the greatness of a tragic spectacle. He left the place, his skin bristling in desperation.

The street was deserted and silent; it grew moister drop by drop; the darkness grew thicker and thicker, and over there on the horizon, the heavens met the earth.

As Robinson walked, he talked to himself:

Death becomes beautiful for the poor; it is better to abandon life and not becomes a slave to voracious appetite with no food.

The six o'clock siren blared out.

Now he was walking stock- straight and at a moderate speed, without realizing that he was in his neighborhood.

The hunched-over houses made artificial walkways; they seemed like they were hanging from threads.

When he got inside his house, he exchanged silent glances with her.

The globe's Forgotten Ones

The pack mule left the sandpit pulling the cart behind it, diligently and without a packsaddle, crossing through an Alamo grove that adorned the space with cool, transparent shade.

The sweat broke out on the animal's hide and the driver's forehead: He mushed the beast insistently, eagerly while Roque pleaded in a low voice:

"If you keep up like that, the mule's going to break."

He chewed his words.

The jockey tried to flash a dry smile, but the attempt floundered in his teeth. He kept silence until it was his turn to get his bearings.

"Is it far?" he inquired in a fake-sounding tone.

"No," Roque answered. "You can go in that way," he said.

He turned onto a sparsely traveled street with inhabited and uninhabited houses, air-conditioned to cool down the high temperature and with terraces of potted shrubs and colorful tables with rosebush vases.

The street was wide and the path was clear. The growing silence stood out. They turned onto another street, on the other side of the residences, and came to a plain piece of flatland. There was nothing new in the neighborhood, except the hovels which were not there, but which could spring up any night with a new tenant inside.

The mule-man team ended were a mason was putting the final touches on a foundation, which held in its center a hut; it was Roque Medina's hut.

"This is it," he said, getting out of the cart.

The rider, stern and silent, emptied the material off one side, stretched his hand out, and pinched the thirteen pesos that Roque gave him; gloomy and sweaty he squinted through the sunrays at him.

"The trip's long and the payment are too little!" He said in his protean manner.

He stared at the mason with the disdain of an unsatisfied "rich man," got on his mount and left as if he suddenly resented his mule.

The mason's eyes followed the rider, who was becoming a black speck on the horizon. Weighing his move, he modestly questioned Roque, who was also watching the rider leave.

In the rear barracks, the children whimpered, pot-bellied from parasites. The older ones played with a bat and a ball.

The dirt pathway looked blurry, and Roque knew why. His wife was blowing a clay bean pot inside the hut.

It was Friday at half-past eleven; Rene has prolonged screams were disturbing Dorita. In three years of concubinage, they had had two children. The first diet when it was barely a month old… yes, they hurried to find something to replace it with so that she wouldn't feel alone, and now their little Rene'! Shared their unlucky existence.

"Shut up, Rene'! We'll be eating right away," he said to comfort him.

The sky was like ivory.

The sun was breaking loose with its molten, torturing rays.

Their everyday reflexes made them take on different tasks.

Surprise!

Yes, a man was running desperately.

"Put everything away, the cops are coming, the lieutenant on the beat," he yelled until he disappeared behind a hovel.

There was no time to interpret what the man meant before the lieutenant said:

"Stop construction."

The mason was annoyed. He did not seem to understand until he saw Roque come into the hut.

The official studied the mason, puzzled.

"You look like a prisoner we had was over there these past few days," he said, clearly wanting to annoy him.

Roque returned to the lieutenant's side. They stared hard at each other.

With the greatest calm, he made it clear:" Don't forget; you and the captain sold me out."

It was a short reply; the official tasted and gulped, but did not his cool. He knew he had made himself understood. Roque's salute confirmed it. He was so content he even winked at him.

The man had wanted to be friendly, and gripping the lieutenant's hand, he left five pesos wadded up in it.

A scorching wind started blowing. The official climbed into the vehicle, which awaiting corporal started. They left behind a black cloud. Roque, blushing, pounded his fist into his open palm.

"Carajo! How long?" He said, his voice breaking furiously.

The mason bowed his head. He felt like crying.

Roque Medina was the night watchman for a private company. It had been a month since he had time off; that Friday was his day off and…well, the truth is he had martyred himself enough. Over time, he'd set out to have something, even if it were only a meaningless barracks, arancheta or hut, in short anything like that humble quarters let him save on the rent he used to pay.

The plot of land? The same question as always; that plot of land he lived on was supposed to be his a year and six months ago.

When they built the housing project in front, the captain and lieutenant were put in charge of watching the plots; they thought they would reward themselves by making a few extra cents.

All coveted the land; the inconvenience was that nobody could invade it because State property is "respected."

Like good brothers, and taking into account that "the boss doesn't bother with it," the captain and lieutenant agreed to sell a few plots of land and swore that no buyers would be harassed. That same day, they were waiting for the solution to a short-lived annoyance. That is what the mason thought.

The afternoon came round with no news. They had eaten, and after a long break went back to work. I was not hot anymore, and the sun was disappearing into the horizon. They found out later that they'd altered his mortar, seized his rods, and demolished a wall; the mason had stopped, flushed when he found an agent had cleaned a plop of mud stuck to the patrol car with a shirt that belonged to his cousin, the foreman of the construction site.

There were no comments. The night made its appearance, and with it the moon, smiling and round as a wheel of cheese, showing off its glow.

Dorita prepared eggs with eggplant. They had supper and rested in bed

The crickets whirred their chirr, chirr, from the humid herbs in the droning night – time chorales; there was a sudden silence.

It was eleven thirty in the evening and suddenly a silence, then immediately a noise, not crickets. This time it was the captain, who like an absolute despot, unyielding and assisted by a patrol, and dedicated now to destroying huts.

They are all desperate: children and women cried.

Some whom courage had not deserted told him off:

"Qué cojones, captain. You sell us out and then command the brigade that leaves us without a roof over our heads."

The captain played the fool and ignored his reply. He threw a woman who lunged at him to the ground; after intimidating the would be arguers, he said:

"The first one to say I sold him out gets ten years."

All you heard now was the stomping and sled-hammer blows his sidekicks carried out on the rooftops. The idea of breaking everything had hit the captain a few days earlier when a man approached him and said he needed the plot to close off a ranch. He showed him the deed, gave him a "loaded" handshake, and everything was fixed.

The rooftops were stroking the ground by now, and the men were thoughtful. The questions came up in their minds:

Why this selfishness when we are all going to die?

When will we poor have some peace on this Earth?

Then they thought about the Moon and the other planets.

The patrol car had driven away and silence invaded the ruins. Someone lost in time spoke up:

"Will the justice we've hoped for all these thousands of years come?"

With this question in mind, they huddled up with their essentials, lay their backs on the planks, and covered themselves with the stars.

SEALED PACT

Superstitions became customs, and custom habit in that small town; after the jefe's fall, you could walk around freely; Saturdays, the Blind Man's bodega was the farmhands and landholders' meeting place.

They listened to native music there, played dominoes, and were never without a bottle of solera, that famous rum, on the table.

The day was foggy and harsh; a thick chilling breeze whistled sharply.

The men guffawed; the mists rained in through the cracks in the gate.

An isolated, indifferent man was drinking the most expensive liquor: Rosendo Fulcar, whose presence was absent before Juan Valerio, with his voice breaking from the surprise, exclaimed:

"God's alive!" Standing there, stunned, and looking in the nook that Rosendo occupied.

Don Rufino Tejeda and his eager assistants had not caught on: They were hubbub about what Juan had said, and one of them exclaimed quietly:

"Compadre, don't tell me God's going to be drinking with us!"

Juan Valerio was quiet. He grabbed the bottle, guzzled drink, and then backed it up by pinching himself to persuade himself that what he was seeing was true.

"Rosendo comes and drinks all by himself," he exclaimed with a certain enthusiasm.

Rosendo had been absent from this lively assembly for only two weeks. The last time they had seen him, he showed up rowdy and loaded with money. He became everyone's drinking host.

That afternoon some commented among themselves:

"Where did he get money from?"

The question had come up in the past: He had beaten his wife and taken the money she made washing clothes.

His problem was that he was a career drinker, and his interest revolved around giving rum to all those present.

From then on, it was enough to smell the bodega's perfume, which he used from the time his life had changed, and all his drinking cohorts jumped all over him.

It started one Saturday afternoon. I was in the bodega watching the chips being tossed around in the markers game, dominoes. It was a new excuse I had just to look into the Blind Man's daughter's eyes. Rosendo was showing off bravery and skill and delivering an angry oath in which he expressed a desire for some business to the devil. The problem was that the Blind Man had denied him a shot.

"You always ask for credit: You owe me one shot already. I cannot give you any more credit.

Rosendo, looking somewhat hazy and if talking alone, said:

"A poor man is a poor man." He was a slave to the vice. He sadly watched him walk away.

That night, the wind's murmur spoke in a low voice; the trees with their long tentacles looked like still and lucid men.

Far off, you could hear the wolves, sorry, the packs of wild dogs, howling clearly.

Rosendo, short, walked slowly among the small static pebbles on the path. The pathway was narrow. You might say a solitary soul in the deep shadow of the night. He looked at the shrubs and a person appeared a voluptuous epicurean delight, which he contemplated. He thought to associate her with someone he knew, a handsome woman with a smiling semblance.

Tempted by the shiver of foolhardiness, he greeted her openly:

"Good evening." Not about to give it any slack, he added: "It's a pleasure for me to share this with the lady."

He got another dry smile. The eyes of a neglected succubus looked at him dead on. Rosendo felt impetuous.

Without a single word more, he took her in his arms and kissed her silently.

He felt a pair of hot and sticky lips, a brutal strength squeezing him; he tried to break loose but couldn't.

The woman? Then said in a gravelly and masculine voice:

"I'm sent by someone you want to make a pact with."

Rosendo felt his curly hair curl tighter, and his skin got goosebumps. The fear now was enormous.

A knot in his throat kept him from speaking. He blushed, his small eyes, his eyewitnesses, wanted to break out of the orifices where they made their homes; then… he muttered with a body length shiver:

"But I…"

The woman cut him off.

The heterogenic spirit was clear: "You called my master and I'm here with his spirit."

"Uh…fine, what I want is money," said Rosendo, armed with bravery and greed.

"Your wife and daughter are the price," exclaimed the woman, who at one moment looked like a damsel, and other like an unkempt old hag and then, like a motley colored animal.

Fear and indecision came to him again. However, greed won over. Rosendo answered:

"The pact…is sealed." Also, from that moment his position changed.

When Rosendo awoke, it was three o'clock in the afternoon; a cold breeze invaded the room through the open window at the head of the bed. He got up calmly and went to the bodega. He was alone by now, for his wife had died recently and no sooner had he recovered from that blow than his daughter was gone. No other event had hurt him as much in his life as what Ligia said on her deathbed:

"You're bad: You traded us for money." She closed her eyes and went to sleep down forever on her bed.

Regrets were biting at Rosen do's conscience, and his losses traumatized him. What good was the money if his loved ones weren't around?

Two nights before her death, Ligia dreamt that the Devil called her and said:

"You're going to be together with your mother; your souls are paid for"

All this brought made her reprimand her father on her deathbed.

The first days, the boys in the neighborhood and the older neighbors commented in the chorus about the mysterious deaths.

Now, Rosendo Fulcar was insolated, with a weapon on the table. He grabbed the pistol with his right hand, ready to shoot himself.

Juan Valerio stepped back, thunderstruck, all at once. He put it on his forehead and squeezed the trigger, the grayish encephalic mass jumped out one side. Immediately his body was covered with a blazing flame. In a second, the prolonged fire scorched the bodega. Only a few of us were able to escape.

"What last longest in us?" The pregnant memory of the green eyes the daughter of the Blind Man had.

VIOLENCE AT THE SCHOOL

"Welcome," said Mr. Fecund to the new teachers that reported to work to P.S. 2000. He was the principal and he felt very worried about the school's history of violence. He thought if he kept a good relationship with the professorship and staff, if he could make the workgroup, he should have better control of the intellect.

Twelve years ago, he was appointed as principal of this school. In the first year, he did not have any trouble with the assignment, but now something horrendous had been happening in the schools of the city. The climate will not be an advantage; the neglect of any one person has been the bigger obstacle to resolving the basic sociological behavior problem.

Mr. Fecund was liked in the school where he worked.

He knew the importance of increased discipline. It would be a great benefit for the schooling community--- and special privilege in his direction--- if he could create his topic and promote the program for other schools, which would recognize him, along with understanding from the system.

He would be called to win the respect of the community and its praise, to have it see the value and prosperity of his successful school. However, without the support from his teachers, it would be too hard for him to implement his ideology.

Mr. Fecund remained at Assembly with his new professorship "I need to count on all of you with your professorship experience to help decrease the condition of violence in our school system and to help to increase the study level."

Unexpectedly, someone cried out "Mr. Fecund!

You want to fight by nothing!"

Mr. Fecund followed by talking about his worries and concerns. He had been renowned as a peacemaker.

Again, from the assembly someone else, ready to excite with treachery and nourish the hate, said:

"Fecund! What do you want? Why do we need to make the change? Man, forget about it. Do you not understand that some people like peace and others love violence?"

Mr. Fecund, wisely, did not dispute the claim of the auditorium member. He knew that his words had caused the desirable effect.

The auditorium was full of confrontations.

"Shut up," shouted another at the same time. "You are a good speaker, but, think… You may be wrong, Mr. Fecund."

Someone else said: "Some people like to abuse from power. And when victims do defend themselves, out sprouts violence."

"Who's ignorant?" asked another member of the auditorium.

"All humans," answered a man.

Mr. Fecund started to feel disillusioned.

"Please, please…"

The same man that sparked the disagreement interrupted Mr. Fecund.

"You aren't good, we don't need to change."

There was a short silence in the auditorium. Soon a green bottle was thrown at Mr. Facund. More confrontation. Many people shouted at the same time. They ran and ran between the chair lines. More and louder cries.

The rehearsal was not going as well as they hoped.

Above the stage, Mr. Fecund, an honorable peacemaker, was showered in blood. He had been seriously hurt!

The goodness of Mr. Fecund was not respected or acknowledged by the auditorium. The people shouted terribly and grew violent. It was sadly demoralizing.

The next day, early in the morning, the newspapers showed on the front page the headline: "DISILLUSIONED AND DISCREDITED."

"Great irony the broken skull of Mr. Fecund, worthy peacemaker, for his speech against violence."

The population observed a moment of silence. Instantaneously, a change of weather darkened the day, and the rain buried the peace.

SECOND PART

THEATER

THE LACKEY'S DECEIT

(MONOLOGUE)

CHARACTERS: TOM

In this work, we will find elements that cannot be translated to the stage. For this very reason, the actor and director will have to dig deep into their imagination in order to create a good production.

It is indispensable to take into account the different imaginary characters the actor will interpret, as well as the change of voices.

A young man of indefinite age enters. He is between adolescence and maturity. He runs quickly, while voices from the grid get louder and louder.

Voice 1: Do not let him getaway!

Voice 2: Stop him, stop him, and stop him!

They get quieter and quieter. The character is still running. He runs into another imaginary character, apparently a woman.

Tom: Hey! Hey! Over there…. You, woman. (*He points at the tip of his tongue with his finger.*) Get out of my way!

He pushes her and walks over her. He keeps running. The voices are heard again coming from the grid.

Voices: stop him, stop him, and stop him!
Silence.

Tom appears in the forest; he continues running until he cannot be seen. When the danger is past, he comes out of his hiding place looking worried; he inhales deep and long, peering outward and side to side as if to search for someone.

Tom: Oh! I lost sight of him! (*A nightingale chirps, other birds sing.*) The birds in the country sound was so beautiful…. It is as if their song brings me peace… (*He doubles over.*) However, no, the heat drives me crazy.

(*Tom hears a noise, like a river running next to where he is. He points his ear to the ground to hear well. He feels his body shudder right away. He takes a few steps; wasting no further time, he decides to strip but is afraid the audience will show some reservations. He rolls up his pant cuffs, takes off his shirt and shoes. He jumps into the river, swims peacefully until he hears another noise, but this one is like the crunch of a crocodile attempting to attack him. Tom swims desperately to the edge and comes out cursing. He grabs a rock and throws it at the reptile.)*

Sheesh! There is no peace anywhere on earth! I am out in the country, the mosquitoes such my blood…. Still, it is worse in the city: I cannot go out into the street because even that bothers some people. Now I come to the river, and this crocodile runs me out.

(*He paces.*)

I do not know what to do. Damn it! I am going to the city even if I have to stay hiding….

(He dresses and exits. He is worried. He varies his steps, first, slow, then running; we hear the sound of lively music.

(*Car horns.*)

(*To audience*) I finally get here, I start to feel uncomfortable. The city is swarming with whore-house and corruption; I am in pain about my brothers, too, but neither you nor I am the proprietors or executors…You are upstart intruders… Are you imported from the fields? Do not get mad at me …I did not mean to offend you … I am just asking.

(Another noise is heard, this time a siren. Tom covers his ears and stretches.)

That sound bothers me. I cannot be in peace, what I said I hear everywhere. Nevertheless, I have not done anything. They only follow me because I shake my head; the problem is they do not believe me… fine, I will tell them, so they can hear it…

They won me over with deceit, offering me work, everything was going to change, and the people would not go hungry… They call that woman Do-ña because she mortifies folks.

(Tom imitates the character who tries to persuade him, giving him a hunchback's waddle.)

You know; you will not suffer anymore, work is an opportunity for man, and it will not be lacking for you.

In his voice)

Until he convinced me. What a job, as if I were some kind of killer for hire. When I agreed to give him my support after I saw him mistreat someone. I tried to ask about it. I paced up and down in the room, indecisive and jittery, my heart sounds like a watch's tick-tock.

(*He imitates a clock, and then he wanders from one side of the stage to the other.*)

Should I ask, should I not ask, should I ask, or should I not ask? Then I made up my mind. Uh, I do not care. I will ask… However, I did not realize the one of the hotty-totty bourgeois was coming into the room. He surprised me.

(*Once again, he imitates the character and is "surprised."*)

You seem very nervous. What do you want to know?

(*Tom shakes his head, now in his voice.*)

Who, me sir?

Who else would it be, is anyone else here with us?

(*Tom is confused.*)

Well, if it is me I want to know anything about it.

What do you mean nothing? Let us hear the question unless you want to lose the tip of your tongue before your time.

Fine, I wanted to ask you something, but I do not know if it will please you.

(*The imaginary character lights up a cigar and smokes.*)

Why not? Everybody in the world has the right to express what they feel, as long as the words you say are we-measured.

I assure you they are well measured, which you can't see, but they'll move you.
Oh, so… go ahead, then.

(*Shyly*) well. Why do we evil things?

(*The character scratches his head and blows out a puff of smoke from the cigar.*)

It seems to me we are going to have to do without you.

Why, sir?

You are a danger to the organization. You just joined and you want to know too much already.

However, you told me…

Shut up, you have no right to talk.

Giving me no further time, he addressed the other lackeys.

Hey you, come here…

(*The character greets him by stamping on the ground and wiping his hand off his forehead.*)

At your service, sir.

Come closer.

(*He pantomimes whispering a secret.*)

And I restless to know what they were talking about, lent my ear, but I still didn't believe they had such a big conscience, and I came back and stretched… by then I was convinced.

(*Mimes cutting his throat.*)

They wanted to silence me. When I was desperate and did not know what to do, I saw the door handle shining like a piece of silver and I jumped up, opened it and ran, ran, ran until I lost sight of him and came here.

(*As if to a passerby* :) Sir! Yes you, I am hungry. Will you share your k, knapsack with me? ...Yes, let us I see...

(*Looks inside the knapsack.*)

Now, what is this? This is not even enough for you... You best go away and leave me alone with my hunger...

Please, sir, go away.

(*He leaves.*)

That is the best thing he did, go away; poor man, to dig so much and never find anything, I am always wrong...

(*To audience*)

What did we say? (*Thinking*)...Now I remember, yes, the people would not suffer from starvation, and because misery is like a burn, I felt my hunger and the people's hunger, and I accepted like an ignorant man. Do not blame me or laugh at me. Do not look at me like that, either. I accepted because I did not know, and now I realize it, but it is too late, I am a fugitive. They want to silence me because I did not want to continue collaborating with them.

I have done nothing. I swear I am innocent. Why do you laugh at me? Everyone thinks I am lying. You only believe them because they are the power… Ah, I know, you are also one of them, except you are in hiding that is it…

You are all a bunch of Canellas. I should not have trusted…

Yes, I see: For you, strength overcomes reason.

(*Glances from side to side. Tom realizes that someone is approaching, and gets nervous.*)

Oh, excuse me, do not give me away. Here comes one: If he sees me, he will threaten me, mistreat me, and if I answer him sourly, he might even kill me. He is going to kill me: I have to hide, I have to hide.

(*He hides fearfully. In addition, an instant later he re-emerges, slowly and carefully.*)

It is over, he finally, left it is over… Damn these stampedes of human torturers: They mistreat you every way you can think of as if we were all alike…The great part is when the man who gives you orders…: You, and everyone… Is honored, they make people go out and chant slogans, like: "There will be money; a lot of sandwiches are going to be handed out, ah and especially the drinks."

Moreover, anybody who does not know what it's all about gets on over there, confident and excited, then starts to move around and jump.

(*He initiates the character who invites him in and whom assists he starts to leap.*)

Eyyyyyyyyyyyyyyyyyyy!

Until by mistake he slips while cutting his caper, a step in the wrong direction and one of those pine sticks they call… A nightstick hits him on the back; he almost ended up like a donkey with broken bones.

(*He imitates the donkey with broken bones.*)

Ah, maybe now you' are convinced about what I am telling you, just like what happened to a mute, because he had no tongue; he was dancing with his little colored flag:

Eeeeeeeeeeeeeeee.

(*He stops starts to pick something up from the ground, blows kisses, waves the little flag, then continue dancing and swinging his belly. He mimics being kneed by someone.*)

In addition, when they cannot take it any longer, they go plug with the huge elbow. Aha: He gets mad then, and starts to say everything he knows: Too bad, he does not have a tongue.

(*Tom imitates an angry mute; he makes sounds, mimes cutting his throat, hurls the flag down, grabs his belly, starts pointing at everyone, and finally what he had climbed before, he runs back down again and throws it out.*)

They kicking him down back and take out, plug, now with the whole foot … And who knows where the poor fellow is… Maybe the flies know where to find him…I slowly discovered that I was sur-rounded in that pigpen. However, what really made me fall apart was that day the boss participated in person. He was frenetic—

(*He imitates the boss, turns his back to the audience, puts on dark sunglasses, and turns around again, moves his head with a nervous tic.*)

I do not tolerate disobedience. The uncle, the boss of bosses' orders is that such and such should not stand in the way… Moreover, you refused to comply with our orders, which are law.

(*He moves from side to side.*)

Sometimes it is good not to be so prominent... As far as, we could say.

(*He puts the sunglasses away.*)

In addition, the lackey wanted to argue and all... However, But...

He retreated meekly, and...One of those gorillas took him in his arms and hurt him.

(*He imitates the strong beating the weaker.*)

Until he left him on the ground. Me? I was afraid; you had to agree with the man, ooooh...

(*He makes the gesture of someone squeezing his own neck, sticks his tongue out like a hanged man.*)

A short time after the columnist one day published---

(*He imitates the columnist writing on his typewriter, then a newspaper boy' a pitch.*)

Extra! Extra! The Director of... Prevaricated with—

(*He imitates the felony with his hand.*)

He appeared sleeping forever in a pool of blood. I felt the need to escape, and that is why I asked: Why do people do evil things? That is why they are running me out.

(*Brief pause*)

I do not know why I complain when they act this way because of me. I collaborated with the man who orders them to persecute me, but I do not fail to admit that it was deceitful, that is why I am not to blame. They said that there would be an overall change for the better, where men could put forth their ideas without fear, but it has not been like that; they lied to me …to live be to choose and to choose is to sacrifice something. I should not complain. I must admit that I have also been desperate.

If a complaint dishonors the tongue, why do I complain? If you put your mind to it, do not accept it or what happened to me will happen to you.

If you are afraid, move away or they will find you next to me.

If you are not afraid, band together because two are better than one.

So then, considering that, not all are equal, and that most are evil, but that is because they pass it on to each other, we will start weeding them out like this:

(*He imitates grabbing and tossing something down in a continuous movement, making sounds as he goes along.*)

Rag, sac, u rag, sac… Tossing them out, until everything is clean. We will live happily after that. Men will love each other, no hatred or evil, what one has belongs to the other.

Moreover, could that be the transformation that they offered me, which they never made good on because you cannot have a new nation without new men… I know that they are strong and hard to beat… It does not matter, a moment ago, I started to feel that I am not afraid, and I notice in every one of your faces that the people's patience is running out.

(*He approaches the audience and takes one audience member by the arm.*)

Are not you afraid... Good, let us go take up against the enemy's weapons... Yes, that is it; take up against his weapons...

(*He nods his head.*)

It is necessary to be free to abolish injustice and rebuild from the rubble of justice...Do not denounce me, even if they offer you money, I am not what you think I am. I am a young man of the people. Believe your conscience and me will be at peace. Good – bye.

(*He tries to go, turns around, and anticipates something.*)

However, do not forget, that the formula for success is in our getting together, each ones of us.

(*He turns his back and goes out running.*)

Curtain.

THE RITE OF REBELLION

Characters:

1. Priest
2. Chandujay
3. Chamba
4. Jerry, the king
5. Robert
6. Gina
7. Chana
8. Man 1
9. Man 2
10. Soldier
11. Woman
12. Guard
13. Voice
14. Men and women townsfolk.

SCENE ONE

The curtain rises. And open air space.

The horizon away. In the downstage area, a group of men and women dressed only in breechcloths. They group before a masked figure that looks like the proverbial devil; it wears a purple rob; it is the High Priest. Loud drums. The high priest executes ceremonial gestures. The drums cease suddenly, and two natives who carry another two men on their shoulders stand next to the high priest.

One is wrapped in a black cloth; the other is dressed like a hunter.

Silence.

Enter a distinguished woman. She kneels next to the priest. She is dressed in a pair of pants and a longs sleeve shirt. The priest takes off his mask, and the persons gathered around kiss the ground, like part of a ritual. The drums play again. When the high priest raises his hand and places it on his chest, they stop suddenly.

Priest: I, the High Priest, representative of the great star that shines upon us, have consulted yesterday at sundown with the glimmer of nightfall, and last night I had my answer. Our divine advisor has said that the election of a king who will manage our affairs and will not remain unaware of the importance of the religious code to put an end to wayward values is pertinent. I have assembled you to tell you about a good vision. We must praise and thank our providence eternally; here:

(He signals to Jerry.)

Our own Jerry-1ro.

The natives rise and applaud him vigorously, clapping, laughing, and jumping. Jerry is placed on the ground, and Robert, the man dressed as a hunter, leaps up off the shoulders of the man who is carrying him. He addresses the natives. The woman who kneeled next to the priest, Gina, rises.

Robert: You must know that the coronation will take place tomorrow, and that we are counting on your support…

We came to this remote place to continue the arduous task started by our ancestors. Therefore, as of tomorrow a fair but strict kingdom will make itself felt. I demand for your good that you leave aside your clumsiness, and proceed to show the wisdom you inherited from our glorious stock.

Humility and obedience will be sufficient indicators to justify your wisdom.

An army has been founded to "protect us from the enemy," which doesn't exist right now but which will come to exist.

This army will take care of the goods in the public domain.

We want cooperation to gather together yellow metals and metals of others colors, to establish a metals fund for the support and sustainment of a kingdom that will never stumble or fall. One day, our motherland will proudly hear of this new world…

(*Brief pause. Sarcastic.*)

"United States of America."

Drums roll. Lights shift, the props people come out on stage. They change the scenery, while three actors move onstage, and the three in chorus:

All: And that is how they foretold our history.

Blackout.

SCENE TWO

Inside of an army barracks. Center stage there is a rustic table with three palm chairs; to one side, a bed of leaves.

Chandujay is lying on the bed resting. Chamba appears stage right with a Bible and another book in hand.

Chamba yells.

Chamba: --- Chandujay, where are you? Are you asleep?

Chandujay: (*Sitting up in bed*)—No. Why the racket, Chamba?

Chamba: I got the books I told you about, and besides I checked Robert's diary.

(*Shows him a thick volume and another smaller one.*)

Look, this a Bible and this is a science book. It is confirmed: They are deceiving many people and have tried to deceive us as well.

(*Shows him a page from the science.*)

80

Look here, the yellow metal is gold and its worth more than life itself to them: The great canoe is called a caravel or ship and it runs with motors.

(*He paces.*)

I wonder: why did the first men teach us their language, and not take care to give us other knowledge?

Chandujay: I will tell you why: Because language was our barrier, and they were not going to get what they were looking for without finding a way to communicate.

(*Pause*)

Tell me how you go about getting these books?

(*They sit at the table.*)

Chamba: Is stole them.

Chandujay: (*A bit surprised*): What?...that is not possible.

You have forgotten that you are not supposed to steal.

Chamba: I know you're not supposed to, but you can.

Don't they want to steal what we have from us?...

They have told us what is good for them, my grandfather told me that his great-grandfather used to tell him: "son, try not to sin, but if you do, try not to let them catch you."

Chandujay: those old men time philosophers: I remember mine used to tell me that overseas they believed in a fair God who had created men in his image and likeness.

Chamba: if that's true, then Satan spawned Robert… I know him well and there is no doubt's he's a bad man. I saw his journal, and I found out he's an anthropologist. He left his country along with others to study, but ever since he came to our island and met us, he's been looking for a way to confuse us so he can take away what we have. Miss Gina is nothing more than his secretary.

Chandujay rises and starts to pace in small circles, nodding his head. He approaches Chamba and taps his shoulder.)

Chandujay: Chamba, you've done well…Now I understand the reason for the king, the army, and everything else… Were there more books where you found these?

Chamba: There are two boxes; one of them has anthropology books, the other has and assortment of things.

(*Chandujay starts pacing again.*)

SCENE THREE

Same scenery as in the first scene. Now stage center there is a throne in which the king will sit; next to that an armed soldier holds a spear and dresses like a Roman soldier.

Men and women come out of every corner, clearing a path through the crowd and all the obstacles in their way. They start bunching together and making comments among themselves. When they reach the throne they stop.

The drums start to play.

The assistants comment aloud on the coronation from backstage. A mestizo, Chana, starts to dance. She wears a grass skirt. Her bodily movements are in sync with the drums. The men feel tempted to touch her. There is improvised combat while Chana keeps dancing.

Taking advantage of the occasion, Chandujay sits down with his back to the throne and facing the audience, and speaks to the men:

Chandujay: That's enough. You don't know what you're doing...

(*Brief silence when his voice is heard.*)

Those men try to confuse us, using subterfuge. God is fair and they're cruel, damaging to our interests, only if we fight as one will we be able to free our selves…

(*Some natives nod their approval.*)

Natives: That's right… that's right.

Chandujay: they use their god as bait so that we, like guppies, fall in their nets and …

(*Robert's voice interrupts him. The king enters stage right accompanied by the priest and two soldiers who carry Jerry.*)

Robert: Guards! Hold that man!

(*The two soldiers leave the king on the ground and arrest Chandujay. He offers no resistance.*)

The men who attended the coronation start to protest.

(*They're silent when the priest speaks.*)

Priest: (*referring to Chandujay*): This man is our Lord's Enemy, therefore he is an enemy to all us.

(*A voice rises in protest from the crowd.*)

Man 1: Yes, the king deserves respect… Down with repression.

Man 2: But how are you going to deprive someone of their freedom when the king's being crowned?

Man 1: We were born like the air like the trees, free as the birds, we ask for them to be released.

All: yes, let them be released.

(*Robert and the priest look at each other. The priest pulls Robert aside and whispers to him*):

Priest: We have to release him until Jerry's crowned.

(*Pause*)

Robert: (*To the men*): Very well, he will be released out of respect for the king…(*To the guards*): Release him.

They release him, and Chandujay mixes in with the audience. Gina, who's been watching everything, smiles with the crown in her hands.

The priest covers his face with the mask and initiates the ritual. He draws water out of a vessel in his hand with a spring of herbs; he scatters it around the throne. He passes the vessel to Gina and takes the crown from her; with a moderate drum roll playing, he holds it out in front of himself. He crowns Jerry king.

The place is overtaken by an outrageous din. In a moment's silence reigns, he slowly rises to the Sovereign's feet; they greet him with reverence and respect.

Jerry, who is sitting on the throne, rises to his feet.

Jerry, people, for the success of this our kingdom it's necessary that everyone contributes with dedication to its happy progress. All ask is that they work a day's work for their future development. (To the soldiers) You are responsible for carrying out the law.

(*Robert smiles maliciously.*)

(The guards don't delay showing off the signs of the king's authority.)

Soldier 1: Let's go. Retreat. You must be rested to face your duties.

Some retire fearfully; others remain behind enthusiastically, motionless, rendering obeisance to the king.

Lights dim.

SCENE FOUR:

Interior of Chandujay cabin. It's nighttime. To the side a candelabrum, the same décor from the second scene.

Chandujay is seated in front of the table. His friends start arriving upstage right; they gather in silence. When they appear to be all together they look at each other curiously.

Chandujay :(*As if passing visual inspection*): Is everyone here?

(*Chana, counting with her index finger, says to herself* :)

Chana: Chamba's missing.

(*Chamba appears from the same place everyone else appears from.*)

Chana: was missing, because he just arrived…

(*He approaches Chandujay.*)

Chamba: I'm sorry for the delay, I was making sure about something they told me. (*He looks him sadly in the eye.)*

Chandujay, my friend, they just hang one of those who were on your side the day of the coronation.

A brief silence and then an irritated murmur is heard among the men; they spit out oaths and angry words.

Brief pause.

Chandujay, with deep sadness:

---- I'm sorry... It's truly painful for that brother to perish because of me (*firmly*) that's one more reason to support the indestructible idea that has brought us all the way here (*they applaud*). If that brother, who did no more than show his fraternal human sentiment for his fellow man, ends up eliminated... then I, who am the one they're looking for, won't get tender caresses they'll try to prevent me from contributing to your general awakening.

Many years ago we thanked those men who with their seed taught us to read and write, but they were noble and perished in the ocean.

To these men who now subject us we owe nothing. They were like missionaries fallen from heaven, but when they learned our weaknesses, blinded by ambition, they turned against us. I'm aware of our ills, I beg your patience, tenacity and good judgment because the moment's drawing near.

The men clap. Gina, silent and smiling, enters upstage right. A murmur is heard again, this time of surprise. Dark skinned woman of remarkable height, quite decisive and furious, stands out from among the group, grabs her by the arm and shakes her.

Chana: (*shaking her*) the hell asked for your prayers, you damned sow?

Gina: (*surprised*): I… Uh…(*Brief pause, now growing furious)*: The priest who officiates at this Mass.

Chana: (*Shaking her*): You'll have to confess if they sent you here to spy.

Gina: (*Trying to break loose*): Let me go, you fool.

(*They grab each other by the hair and roll around the ground.
The men egg Chana on.*)

Man 1: Punch her hard, Chana.

(*Chamba, uncomfortable, break them apart*):

--- That's enough! (*Reprimanding the men*): You should be ashamed of yourselves.

Man 1: If she were a man, she'd slice her neck open. She come to spy on us. She'd came to spy on us.

Chandujay: (*From his place*): No, she's our contact. She came with them, but she's with us.

Chamba: (*Calmly*): You should apologize to the young lady.

Chana: (*Embarrassed*): Oh, I'm sorry miss... You must know how we feel. Just thinking that they kill defenseless people makes me furious. I didn't know what I was doing.

(*She cries and moans. Gina approaches her and runs her hand through her hair.*)

Gina: I understand, darling, we're going to be very good friends.

Chana: (*Looking into her eyes*): Really? (*They hug.*)

Gina: (*To Chamba*): I left the books I'm missing in your cabin.

Chamba: (*Taking her by the shoulders*): Miss, there's no way to pay you back for your altruism.

Gina: The best pay is the trust you've placed in me.

(*Chamba release her and looks at the men*):

Chamba: Are you beginning to be convinced of the young lady's kindness?

Gina: Please make me feel like one of you... call me Gina. To (*Chandujay*): You must aware that the king's guards are looking for you, why don't you hide until everything quiets down?

Chandujay: (*Coolly*): I Know, but I won't accomplish anything by running away from reality. They know where to find me. They can torture me, they can hurt my body, but my ideals stand firm and will grow like the air that we breathe, like the blood that runs through our veins.

Chamba: (*To Gina*): You came with them and support our cause. Why doesn't the priest do the same?... The promised Messiah preached in the name of truth, justice, equality and died for it...Why do you all use the Doctrine to make us believe that God wants us to suffer?... And what I don't understand is why you sacrifice yourself for us.

Gina: Don't wonder that I help you. (*Brief pause, she slowly moves forward.*) My father was a slave to a master as cruel as Robert. From the time I was a young girl, I loved the freedom that later on a good man gave me. I hate masters, I've always hated them. My father preferred suicide to live in humiliation for the rest of his life. (*Now she's excited.*) And I don't want you to suffer the same luck, I don't want that!

Chamba: (*Resolutely*): For the sake of the peace we long for in the world, Death to the Intruders!

(*All in unison*):

All: Death, death, death!

(*The king's guard breaks into the cabin, wielding spears.*)

Soldier 1: In the name of the king, you're arrested.
The surprise throws them into commotion. Everyone runs back and forth. Lights dim.

SCENE FIVE:

The king seated on his throne, two soldiers on either side and one behind him. They're carrying spears and swords in scabbards tied around their waists.

The reception room in the castle is broad in front. Robert, with a whip around in his neck, and the priest, watch a dark-skinned woman dance a morbid rhythm. The space in the center has been cleared to allow the king to see. A few soldiers and women. Once she stops dancing to the rhythm of the drum, the priest takes her by the arm and is about to allow her to fall backward, but when he does so the guards appear. Guard 1: My loyalty to the king has helped me discover the mastermind behind a conspiracy.

(*Jerry, the king, rises.*)

Jerry: Your king will take such a commendable feat into consideration. (*He searches for something among the audience members*). Where is everyone else?

Guard 1: The dungeon is his jewel box.

Jerry: You've done well. (*To the priest*): Lord, in the name of the purity of men with noble ideals, I hope you know how to judge this rebel.

(*The priest puts on his mask and traces strange symbols in the air, then pronounces the verdict*):

Priest: Whereas the detained man committed the crime of inciting a riot, with the purpose of destabilizing the kingdom, he is condemned along with his friends to five years of public works, the lightest punishment in our civilized civilization, and without taking into account his sins.

Robert: The verdict is just and is approved. Bring the bulls in.

(*The soldier's exit.*)

Jerry: (*To Robert*): It must be in the Library.

(*Two soldiers enter with a man in chains. Behind them She comes a woman with wild hair who comes on screaming. She kneels at the king's feet.*)

Woman: Your majesty, my husband wasn't involved in that, forgive him. We have five children, and if he's absent they're going to suffer… We live next to the neighbor's hut (*indicating Chandujay*), but we don't know anything about it, we swear.

Jerry: Neighbor you said?... So much more reason to add to this; you knew about the conspiracy beforehand and you kept it hushed.

(*The woman cries desperately, holding on to one of king Jerry's feet. He kicks her furiously and barks orders out to the guards*):

Jerry: Take the woman out of here!

(*The soldiers obey him. They drag her out. She screams:*)

Woman: You're unjust, cruel, mean and damned to hell!

(*Robert approaches the man and sneers at him.*)

Robert: So, conspiring, hey? (*Furious*) Bastard! (*The man spits in his face. Robert is furious.*) How dare you, you repulsive human being?

(*He whips him, and then wipes his face. The guards enter with the men in chains.*)

Guards: your majesty, here are the prisoners. (*He shows him the men in chains.*)

Jerry: (*marveling cynically*): Oh, they look plenty strong…

(*He gestures with his hand for them to be taken out to begin serving their sentences. The man they brought in behind the woman tries to start an argument.*)

Man: But your majesty, us?

Robert: (*interrupting him*): Silence….

(*Jerry, coming close to the man and giving him a threatening look*):

Jerry: Bastard, you dare speak my name. The man who conspires against me is my enemy (*striking his chest*): Do you understand? (*Now looking at Chandujay:*) How about you? …So you're the mastermind? (*Strikes him in the face*)… You'll pay for your rebellion. (*To the guards*): Everyone to the dungeons. (*To Robert: You know what to do.*)

(*Robert, loudly guffawing and in a sarcastic tone of voice*)

Robert: You are majestic, Yes, I know what I have to do.

(*He unwraps the whip around his neck,cracks it, and continues laughing.*)

Lights dim.

SCENE SIX:

The castle interior. The men are carrying a heavy load tied to a branch and strung from their shoulders. Some can't bear the load, others fall and are mushed on by the pressure of Robert's whip and guard 1's kicks. When they're whipped in the ribs, they crawl along with the floor writhing in pain. They're all shirtless and wear nothing but a breechcloth. A yellow glow of a light precedes the red flashing light. The character's suffering comes out into the audience. A woman who shares the load with one of the men falls on her knees, exhausted; her body refuses to obey her.

Chandujay attempts to help her, the body refuses to obey her.

Chandujay attempts to help her, but when he comes close he runs into Robert, who holds him back and shoves him.

Robert: Get out of the way, son of a bitch!

(*He strikes the woman with the whip. Chandujay tries it again, but two guards take him by the arms and push him aside. Furious, he tells Robert*)

(*He strikes the woman with the whip. Chandujay tries it again, but two guards take him by the arms and push him aside. Furious, he tells Robert*)

Chandujay: Robert, I didn't know that aside from being inhuman you were an abusive coward.

Robert: What did you say? (*He offers a jeering noise with his tongue*): well, well…(*He starts to count off, on his fingers as he enumerates a list*): The brave, the fool, the defender. (*He throws the whip at him*). Let's see how intelligent you are. (*Brief pause.*) Come on, strike her.

(*Yells his demand*): Strike her!

The guard's release Chandujay. He picks up the whip silently, looks at the others, and strikes Robert along the length of his body. Robert writhes.

Robert: Oh, you son of a bitch! (*To the guards: Seize him!*)

The guards obey and struggle until they manage to overpower Chandujay. Robert strikes his face, his belly until he is motionless, lifeless.

Lights dim.

SCENE SEVEN:

Inside of the castle, the throne center stage and the sentries alongside it. Jerry, the king, converses downstage with Robert and the priest.

Jerry: We have to think of a way to resolves the hostilities with these men.

Robert: How? Oh… I understand, by persuading Chandujay to join us. The men listen to him… Besides, he's started this situation and he has to…

Priest: (*Interrupting*): I very much doubt that he will accept a bribe, his liberty comes first.

Jerry: But he doesn't think like a civilized man; he's a fool and altruist who still believe in community values.

His freedom won't be enough when what he's looking for is his people's freedom.

Jerry: (*Angry*): I see we're showing signs of weakness.

There's no time to look back. Why didn't you think about this earlier? Now he hates us as never before.

(*He paces from side to side*) I ordered that he not be fed until he promises to forget everything.

Priest: Even worse. (*To Robert*): He'll have greater reason to nurture his hatred: feed the dog and watch it wag its tail and forget to bite you.

Robert: (*Still annoyed, to the priest*): I always thought you were a good advisor, but don't sweat it, the devil will be able to choose a nice place for you in hell. (*Tapping his *shoulder*) Don't be an idiot, Mr. Priest. Do you believe that after getting a beating he's going to smile at me, even if I give him food?... Come on, they're not deeply asleep anymore. Before, when you drew your symbols in the air, they believed you where the High priest. Now, though, they surprised us when they wake up from an old slumber and I still can't find an explanation.

(*Guard 1 enters holding Gina by one arm, escorted by two soldiers. Gina offers resistance.*)

Guard 1: I can explain it (*indicating Gina*): She fed the prisoner, and for some time has been passing teaching materials on to him behind your back.

Jerry: (*Surprised*): You, Gina? (*pause*) What; you prevaricate? You came here with us and now you tread the path of the felon to harm us. Why?...

(*Gina, who's still held by the arm by guard 1, abruptly pulls loose.*)

Gina: I don't believe I'm prevaricating, or that I'm on the path of a felony. I never said I agreed with what you're doing. You hired me to do secretarial work, not to mistreat folk. Everything was going along well until you had the absurd idea to crown a king who promised to protect the people. They, not knowing your future intentions, gave you all their support and…

Robert: (*interrupting her aggressively*): Enough…(*He approaches her and takes her by the shoulders.*) You're a fool, you are. If you weren't you wouldn't cast away the chance to get rich and stop being such a prim and proper lady.

Gina: (*with uncontrollable fury*): Robert, you're an ambitious beast. (*Tries to break loose*): Let me go.

(*Robert shoves her hard. He straightens out his collar sarcastically as he rearranges himself.*)

Robert: Very well, Ms. Heroine, you just became our Antipode, let's see how long you stand up to torture: Naturally it will start with the death of your courageous friend. (*He laughs.*)

Jerry: (*Insistent, trying to persuade her*): Gina, If you ask for forgiveness we'll be indulgent, and this little incident can easily be forgotten.

Gina : (*unbailable*): I don't want to know anything, don't count on me for your plans.

Priest: (*To Gina*): Coming to this Island Where the language isn't a barrier is a wonder; don't forget that prudence doesn't get you fed.

Gina: (*Cool as the priest*): Don't forget, Mr. imposter, that no providence will forgive your sins; if the outside authorities hear about this, you'll die in jail. (*Pause*)

Robert: (*looking at the priest, at Jerry and then at Gina*): Don't worry, darling (*pointing a finger at her*): You won't live to tell it…(*To the guards*): Take her away. The guard's exit with Gina. (*Robert looks at Jerry again and at the priest*): We'll have to kill her.

Blackout.

SCENE EIGHT:

Night. Pitch black. Inside the dungeon, the men sleep on the floor. A voice is heard inciting to action.

Voice: Calabó bambú, help yourself and I'll help you.

The drums play loudly; a dim green light illuminates the stage. Two men move. Chandujay and Chamba are back to back and loosen each others' shackles; silently they help the others, whisper in their ears; the men, absorbed in thought, stand up, look at each other and dance to the beat of the drum; they sing the chorus the voice sang, improvise, it's a frenzied dance, a kind of orgy. Chana, lying face up on the ground, stirs. Some crawl on the ground in frenetic attack poses. It's the rite of rebellion. Yells are heard at intervals.

On the opposite side of the stage, the light falls on the throne in the background; the sentries are still in position next to the throne. Jerry, Robert, Priest, and Guard 1 pace worriedly back and forth. Faraway voices are heard singing the song the men had started earlier.

Voices: Calabó bambú, bambú, I will be free, help yourself and I'll help you.

It grows closer with each passing second. As the sound of the drums grows:

Jerry: You say they're crawling in the ground?...(*Pause, a deep sigh*) This is a problem! Don't stand there with your arms crossed, do something!

(*Robert and Priest look at guard 1 as if to insinuate something.*)

Guard 1: What? What should I do?... I think I should pull out: I quit all this.

Robert: You quit?... (*Smiles*) You can't do that now.

(*Firmly*) We're in this and we have to stay firm.

Guard 1: You do it, not me.

(*Robert seizes his neck with uncontrolled fury; the guard tries to pull loose in vain. Robert lets the lifeless body sink to the floor. Jerry and the priest now look desperate.*)

Jerry: (*reprimanding Robert*) You shouldn't have done that… We can't go around finishing each other off.

Robert: (*looking at his hands as if delirious*) He was afraid and he needed to be broken. (*Pause*) There will no longer be any treason in fact. (*The drums and voices are heard closer by the minute.*)

(*Now losing his sense of reality*) That devilish noise is directed at us (*cups his ears with his hands, his eyes look ready to pop out of his skull*): I'll struggle against everything, power will be on my side, our greatness, our greatness (*falls to the ground, Pause, crawls to where the guard is*):

I'm afraid, I'm afraid. (*He hugs the cadaver.*): I did it because I'm afraid.

(*He's quiet. Jerry, the king, and the priest look on nervously. The drums sound throughout the scene.*)

Jerry: (*to the priest*): He's crazy!

(*Stage left, surreptitiously, three men move in at the rear, overtake the guards who watch the throne, grabbing them by the neck and bringing them to the ground. They take their respective places. Now, from stage right, Chandujay, Chamba, Chana and Gina followed by the men*).

Priest: (*Uneasy, to the men, advance slowly, silently toward them*): In the name of providence, halt! Guard! Guard!

(He turns to the throne and is surprised to find the "change of guard.") Oh! (*A man steps forward, tries to face down the priest. The priest extends his arm and places it on his forehead.*)

Asps, generation of vipers, staining your hands with my blood will mark your souls for eternal fire in hell. (*He releases the man, who retreats fearfully.*)

Chandujay: Many are the false prophets, who say and do not do, for they tie on you heavy burdens that are difficult to carry and place them on men's shoulders, but those who put them there would not lift even a finger to move them. (*The priest retreats. Chamba takes over the crown Jerry wears. He comes off the stage showing it before he approaches one of the spectators in the first row and crowns him king. A din is heard.*)

The actors who represent the townspeople clasp each other's hands and join in an improvised circle with other spectators. (*They raise their arms above their heads and form a pyramid.*)
(Blackout)

(Curtain)

THE TRIAL OF A CORRUPT AND UNJUST MAN

A Satire in One Act and Three Pictures

Characters:

Mister Gordon

(Expressionist make up)

A man who represents the sun

A woman who resembles justice

(Expressionist make up)

A homeless man

A woman who depicting the conscience.

(Expressionist makeup with distinct colors)

The reflexive lady

The Trial of a Corrupt and Unjust Man

It develops on a country morning, where the birds sing and the love shudders, on the outside of a house some trees in the process of growth, some bushes of flowers and grasses of the savanna, and a leafy tree with flowers in the center of a forest…

(*Outside the scene, in the background, behind the public, appears dispossessed, when the light goes out, without the assistants can notice his presence until he does not intervene*).

Dispossessed (*dressed in rags speaking from the audience*):-- Oh, Lord of the helpless, virgin of the scattered… It was all I could think to say when suddenly I found myself on this façade (*ask someone from the audience*): Do you think that all my life I have been the way I am? (*Pause while waiting for an answer*): well, not, only now I am like a bird without a nest, and always ignore that I had chosen this destiny.

From another side of the stage, sitting among the audience the woman who represents conscience: -- what horror, it can't be, that this is the way that it has to travel! (*In another different side, justice intervenes*).

Woman who represents justice:----- I refuse to accept that destiny, as natural something. (From another corner the presence of the sun stands out).

The Sun:---- However, I lit the balance of destiny.
Conscience: I never imagined that I would come to assist a pervert who would trace him, who would trace patterns to my path.

Reflexive Lady (*to Gordon*):----Surely some time, I thought to tell the world what maybe I loved you, without reality denouncing That I hated you; I made a destiny in my path and that the light came to reflect in each step of my journey… (*Short pause, as if thinking*): Remembering, when the buttons of my chest gushed like a hard funnel, and without my wanting to, you took me to heartbreak and hatred, when in your role as a victim you dese-crated the tenderness of my flesh.

(*A confrontation between Gordon and the Reflective Lady is dramatized, Gordon intends to rape her, the Lady seizes a stick that she finds within reach of her hands.*)----If you approach I'll break this stick in your forehead; I warned him, emboldening me.

(*The Sun and the justice in chorus.*): More he did not care and in the first carelessness, on it was launched, and as he was stronger…(*Indicates the Reflective Lady, remain static, while Gordon and she return to dramatize, they press, Gordon over her slaps her, dominates her and it is seen that he owns her by force.*)

---- Do not try to resist you that I do not want to lacerate you, all that this farm has, it belong to me, including you, to try to reject me is a waste of time. (*Static on the Reflexive Lady*).

The Sun: ---- And noticing it like that, he took it by force (*remains static again*). And after some bushes, without being seen, someone watched, when Gordon insulted her, nerves betrayed him and a cough denounced him, and the Smith and Watson revolver with one-shot cut him off. (*Gordon takes out a revolver and shoots, the dispossessed plays candid, the man he describes and falls shot by the bullet fired by Gordon, who after firing blows the hole in the revolver's cannon, remains static*).

(*The Sun and the justice to chorus*):

-----Poor Candide the peon, violently he died. The Reflexive Lady pushing to Gordon of over her is closed).

Reflexive Lady:-----I was already bled, then I felt disgusted, I felt that I was already dead, ready to bury me, I felt that I had killed myself, that with Candide I was dying.

(*Justice takes off his black glasses and covers his eyes with a black bandage*).

Dispossessed:-----Justice had been blinded, and Gordon's money upset the way (*Gordon shows the public a wad of bills*).

The Sun:-----Before so much pain, the mother of this reflection, went and asked for an explanation, a high price paid, the executioner killed her. (*Justice even with the bandage on*):-----And in a common grave, he has both buried them, without remorse, without feeling that he had sinned.

Conscience:-----I, like his consciousness, felt disturbed; I did, I was remorseful, but I manage my life.

Reflexive Lady:-----In truth, I freaked out, out, and in terrestrial traffic, I escape; and in my pilgrimage I could fly. (*The Reflexive Lady shouts as she rolls on the floor*).

----- AAAAAAhhhhhhhh, I feel that I burn I was disappointed and from the ranch of Gordon, I ran away, to the heavens I flew and now and now that I return to the judgment of that unjust I will join. (*Staying Still, Mr. Gordon, who was paralyzed, begins to move while replying, saying to the sun*):

Mr. Gordon:---- Blasphemy alienates me, and I do not know who are you, do not steal my virtue.

The Sun:---- You lack emotion, you never aspire to forgiveness (*Conscience hardening*).

Conscience:---- Is that I am his emotion, for me, he knew love! (*Says indicating Gordon, while he approaches a man in the audience, lifts him front the seat and strokes his hair.*) --- Is there any motivation?...

(*Gordon frenetic from the position where he had been static*):---- I forbid you to flirt that stranger.

(*The surprised and frightened conscience returns to the stage while replicating*):

Conscience:---- Until I started to feel hostile.

(*The dispossessed approaching the conscience, begs*):

-----: Please have mercy on me.

(*Mr. Gordon to the Dispossessed*):----- It in vain that you scream and cry, she belongs to me. (*Laughs out loud*):-- Hahahahahaha.

(*The Dispossessed retreats with a certain fear*):---- But I just wanted…

Mr. Gordon: ---- Do not insist fool.

(*The Dispossessed remains static.*)

The justice: ---- After everything caused he wanted to overlap it.

The sun:--- But, I was aware.

(*Shouts are heard as from beyond the grave*)

The Dispossessed:--- The dead from their graves claimed justice.

Reflective Lady:---- But Gordon made fun (*Gordon laughs out loud, while the others stay static, he goes to the audience*):---- With my money I buy everything I want, a wagon, a drinker, and a filly that gives me consolation.

(*He slaps the Reflective Lady on the buttocks and laughs, while she makes a rejection gesture*).

Mr. Gordon:--- Hahahahahahahaha.

Justice:---- With such arbitrariness, not one will live in peace, and I felt worried. (*He moves from side to side as showing concern*):--- Suddenly, a ray of light, I grant the solution.

(*The Sun approaches justice and surrounds it with its mantle, they remain static.*)

(*The Dispossessed and the Reflective Lady take each other's hands as they kneel.*)

Reflective Lady takes:---- We prayed to the saints(*They just kneel, facing each other emitting murmurs as if in prayers, Gordon pours himself a glass of wine, tastes it and pours the contents into the face of the dispossessed*).

The Reflective Lady:----We kept praying->(*They pretend to pray, then the Reflective Lady remains static, the Dispossessed wiping her face*):--- And Gordon was still mocking.

(*Gordon laughs out loud as he leaves the stage*).

The Sun:---- And earthly justice, never found cause against your money; and Heriberto (*indicates the Dispossessed*):-- That nothing possessed, I cry to divine justice at the time, (*justice takes off the bandage*).

The Dispossessed:--- And so it was that I looked and saw, they all pleaded for me.

Justice:----- Yes, and it was like that, I turned his guardian anger and his defender went.

(*The justice embraces the Dispossessed*).

The curtain closes.

It develops at dusk inside a house; to one side a table and some chairs, a large hanging portrait, in the division of the central side, in the same location, when the curtain was opened, Mr. Gordon dressed in a coat and tie, dozing reclining in an old piece of furniture; feet on a small table without vase.

(*The Sun, dressed in yellow, and illuminated by clear light, makes symbolic pirouettes that give the impression that it emits rays towards the public*):

The Sun:---- It all started one afternoon when I was faced with a weighted Mister. (*Untimely there a light change and the action moves to the scenes where Mr. Gordon slept, who appears illuminated by a reddish light, first on one side, then shifts position, and begins to fall asleep. after a pause, wakes up instantly*).

Mr. Gordon:--- My money, my money. (*He looks back and forth, pinches himself.*) Oh, so much the better, it was just a nightmare. (*pause. He approaches the apron and talks to the audience*). I was falling asleep and saw and intruder robbing me. (*Brief pause, to someone break into my house?*) No?

(*Brief pause, and frenetic reaction*). Careful with being an accomplice because I won't tolerate it, I won't tolerate it.

(*He sits and falls into a position of deep thought.*) Stage right, under white light, the man who represented the Sun. He moves slowly, dressed in bright yellow. He watches Mr. Gordon silently before he speaks to him.

Man who represents the Sun: Good afternoon.

Mr. Gordon: Do you know who I am? (*Mr. Gordon rises suddenly*) Uh, who are you? How did you get in here?

(*The Man who represents the Sun with serenity*): I come to asks you to account for yesterday.

Mr. Gordon (*Surprised*): What?... Uh, uh...Are you a thief?

The Sun: What makes you think that?... And if I were, does someone who has no morals have any right to demand morality?... Who's more guilty in your eyes, the innocent person who's blamed for a crime or the executioner who, to drive his pride home, uses his power to blame a scapegoat?
Mr. Gordon: So stop going into philosophies I don't understand and get down to brass tacks. What are you talking about; I don't understand what the big deal is about yesterday.

The Sun: You don't know?

Mr. Gordon: No.

Man, that represents the Sun: Besides being greedy and cruel you're cynical, hypocrite and inconsiderate.

Mr. Gordon (*spiteful*): Out of my house! Who do you think you are to come in here and disrespect me? Out, out of here!

Man who represents the Sun (with serenity): I am the source of all clarity. I represent the star of light. From my pores issue the energies of purity and truth. I am the Sun.

Mr. Gordon: What? (*Brief pause. He laughs loudly, pointing to the man who represents the Sun, who gives away certain complicity with the audience*) you're crazy; he says he's the Sun! (*Keeps laughing.*)

The Man who represents the Sun places his hands on his temples as if to concentrate. He transmits burning rays into Mr. Gordon's body, which stops laughing when the rays make an impact on him and start to roll around desperately.

Mr. Gordon:---- (*Still crawling*): Y, y….yyy… You are the Sun, I can't believe it!... What ….What do you want?

Sun: I told you already, to ask your account for your cruelty.

You'll have to take it back anyway; your power and money won't do you any good before heavenly justice.

Mr. Gordon: Why?

Man who represents the Sun: Because it will also ask you to account for your sins.

There's no excuse for your having someone hanged that gave their youth to you and took care of your castle, just so you wouldn't have to retire him and could take over his pension.

Mr. Gordon (*Defiant*) You're misinformed. You're twisting around the core truth. why don't you just say that that wretch wanted peaceful rest because he'd accumulated an unplayable debt, and I don't know how or why, because I paid him the necessary wages for him to live? I'd call him privileged because he grew old working for me, making money, and he was so ungrateful that he even got the rope he hanged himself with on credit and so selfish that he died without paying me back.

Sun: Confess the truth, it will make it easier for that grand jury up there if you tell them that you paid him the necessary wages for him to die and since he didn't die, you had him lynched.

Mr. Gordon: falsehood of all falsehoods; you have a gimmick to make me believe that you're the Sun, and you almost tricked me, because the Sun is as cruel as the cruelest, and in that, you resemble the Sun that burns men's skin.

Sun: I'm not cruel. My rays awaken the conscience of men.

Mr. Gordon: conscience…(*Brief pause*) Coño! This gets messy. I knew he was a communist.

Sun: Silence. That expression has been banned from the Earth. It shall not be named or applied where there is selfishness or despotism, the expression is a divine term Satan took from the Garden of Eden to confuse the Godson's. Your description, however, will last a long time: Landholder, corrupt, upstart and heir.

Mr. Gordon: So, what's wrong with that? (*Brief pause*) I won't have another word with you. I came to his country as a child, that's why I'm from this country. My parents earned what they invested, so I'm an heir by law: Besides, all my lands are planted except for a few lots that were reserved for cattle grazing.

Sun: That's all fine. But if you want to feel joy in your conscience, you must resort to a practical utopia, which is when you distribute among those who have nothing and who have helped you so long to strengthen your fortune and make it grow, all those virgin lands you own and which you aren't using.

Sun: That's all fine. But if you want to feel joy in your conscience, you must resort to a practical utopia, which is when you distribute among those who have nothing and who have helped you so long to strengthen your fortune and make it grow, all those virgin lands you own and which you aren't using.

Mr. Gordon: (*Hysterical*) Madman, madman, madman, out of my sight, if they were yours you wouldn't even suggest such a folly (*to the audience, as if he were requesting its support or approval*): The problem is that they're never happy. I've been paying them a salary that few have the privilege of receiving (*now facing the Man who represents the Sun*). I'm the one who pays the best: everyone else pays two pesos, and I pay two and a half a day, just for doing a simple task: Milk the little cows and while they're at it they rub the udders of the best cows in the country.

Sometimes I get the idea that they rub them with their feet and milk them with their mouths because the milk doesn't go far. (*He thinks*.) Yes, (*pause*) How come I didn't think of this before? Damn it! They're stealing from me.

(*Yelling*) They're stealing from me! (*Lowers his voices*) Ten long Years losing money. I would have enjoyed it more in in the bank than giving it to those men, who badmouth me now.

Man the represents the Sun: Don't forget that the Earth is not a decorative object, therefore it should belong to those who work it: true wealth isn't just about "possessing the treasure", but how it's used. In the same way that the Sun shines for all, with its clear rays, God announces and assigns the right to life to each living thing.

Mr. Gordon: (*Frenetic*) That's none of your business! Out of here! Ahhhhh; I hate you.

Sun: (*walking away*) I make you understand what I must. Remember: There will be no peace for your conscience as long as you prefer to see your lands turn to stone than let needy people work them, see your unused clothing turned to cobwebs before letting the homeless wear them, see your money sitting idle in between planks instead of investing to help other people and develop your country… I believe your conscience will never leave you in peace. (*Exits*).

(*When the man who represents the Sun exits, Mr. Gordon watches in silence. He jeers at him and a hateful expression comes over him. Aside*:)
Mr. Gordon: Insolent Sun, you sting men's eyes and then talk about conscience. (*He cups his hands next to his mouth as he looks for a way to express himself and almost yells, defiant*): My conscience is clean!

Blackout.

A single light cast on the space where the Dispossessed crawls. He moves slowly to the side where justice and the Man who represents the sun are standing. He moves in a circle: When he's in front of them he speaks:

Dispossessed: Judges of my cause, celestial spheres; I am the homeless man who worked my bones to a pulp on Godon's (*pause*): Justice, justice to affirm the hopes of the honest people, don't let anyone call you a blind woman in my case… (*The woman who Represents the Justice makes a note in her notebook looks at the Dispossessed and exits accompanied by the Man who Represents the Sun. The Dispossessed continues with his speech.*)

Sun, who lights up the path of men, justice who shall break the corrupt hands of those who alter you, don't prolong my pain. (*Grabs his stomach.*) Hunger wracking my stomach, stop knocking at my door.

Mr. Gordon and the Woman who Represents the conscience come on stage. She is dressed in black. Mr. Gordon laughs hysterically. He's carrying a hard rubber stick and a stool, which he places stage right while he orders Conscience, with gestures, to sit in front of the stool. He approaches the Dispossessed who retreats in fear.

--- No…

(*He grabs the Dispossessed and places his head on the stool.*) Conscience kneels as she pounds herself on the chest.

(*Mr. Gordon hits the Dispossessed with the stick.*)

Mr. Gordon: why do you ask to be freed of the favor I did for you?... You were born to be the way you are.

The woman who Represents the conscience back-stage replies:

Conscience: No, that's not true.

Mr. Gordon (*a surprise to be questioning his conscience*): What… you are my conscience and you dare contradict me!

Woman who represents the conscience: You're so unfair that you falsely accuse your conscience. I didn't say a thing.

Mr. Gordon: No! (*He storms about the stage. A brief pause; Conscience thinks, takes the Dispossessed in her arms and silently caresses him, Mr. Gordon is even more surprised.*): You think you're going to drive me mad, you just contradicted me and now you deny having done it.

Conscience: Even black like this, I can make you blind! Remember; I am your Conscience and I will always be a part of you.

Mr. Gordon: (*smiling*) So you're on my side.

Conscience: You know I am…at least as long as you're moderate, nothing will stand in your way. I'm strong and I can't be bitten, I'm like Lucifer's conscience.

Conscience Exits, laughing.

Mr. Gordon: (*Trying to keep her there*) Wait, uh… Moves from side to side, worried, stop abruptly, pause.): Oh, this is enough to drive you mad. (*Pause. Thanks.*) Yes, I'm convinced, there's only one guilty person, the villain who pretends to be the Sun, why does he have to stick his nose in things that aren't his business? There is no cause for him to reprimand me because everything I possess is mine. (*Raising his voice as if to defy the audience.*): I do whatever I please with my inheritance, whatever, anything I want. (*Jeers and laughs heard offstage. Mr. Gordon moves around desperately and unsuccessfully trying to find where it's coming from. He angrily addresses the Dispossessed Man who's still on the floor.*) You're guilty too, you filthy pig, I'll kill you.

He tries to strangle him. Conscience enters and comes between them.

Conscience: Don't be a fool. Something terrible has happened.

Mr. Gordon: (*Surprised*): What do you mean?

When Conscience tries to explain to him stage left, the man who represents the Sun enters and threatens him.

Man who Represents the Sun: Silence. Don't try to explain anything to them; this man's more stubborn than a wild mule. If you keep this up I'll burn you.

Woman who Represents the Conscience: (*indecisive and afraid:* ---- I… I'm…!

Man who Represents the Sun: You choose between the banner of glorified exaltation and a rotten abyss. (*To Mr. Gordon*) I'm still waiting for a simple answer. Will you give your surplus riches to the poor, or will you persist in oppressing people?

Mr. Gordon (*In a frenzy*): Never! Over my dead body! You're a thief!

Man who Represents the Sun: What good will your riches do if you die tomorrow?

The satisfaction that treasures bring is not in possessing them: Its unfair, I'm telling you again, for you to deny security, health, and well being to those who give their lives to you to swell your fortune. If you practice doing good you'll be happy.

Mr. Gordon: I'm happy in my way. Don't keep trying to change me, my servants are my servants, that's what I pay them for. Try to understand, they're my employees, not my children. Leave me alone, I have not children, I'm happy loving my money.

Woman who Represents the Conscience to (*Mr. Gordon*): You're hugely wealthy, they'll help you build a solid empire. I don't see it as a bad thing for you to distribute a percentage of the surplus.

Mr. Gordon (*more angry*): You're my conscience but you don't sound like a good one to give advice. You're banned of the right to suggest anything to me.

Woman who represents the conscience: If that's how you're going to be, don't count on me, I can't support you. I'm leaving. Everything will be left behind when you leave.

(Mr. Gordon steps aside now, and he looks nervous, desperate).

Mr. Gordon: No, you can't leave me; (*he touches above his heart*) I don't feel well, I need to go to the doctor. (*He tries to go out, but justice blocks his path.*)

Woman who Represents Justice: That's not necessary. There's no better doctor than your conscience, without it you'll be like an empty body, unreasoning, a restless peace less lunatic…it's too late, your properties were confiscated, they'll be held until the light of truth floods your conscience.

Mr. Gordon: What!...No, it can't be. (*Yells*) No o o! (*Crumples over*).

Conscience, surprised, looks at the Man who Represents the Sun and the Woman Who Looks Like Justice. She kneels in front of Mr. Gordon's body, moves it from one side to the other.

Woman who Represents the Conscience: Oh, no. He's dead. (*Looks at the Man Who Represents the Sun again.*) He can't stand the weight of justice.(*The Dispossessed gets up slowly, staggering toward the apron, facing the audience.*) That's how men end up, the little we are is what we do, though the wealthy frequently make their deaths a matter of showing off their vast knowledge, and they die from ulcers, cancer and mistrust.

Reflective Lady:--- Human beings before birth we choose things different from those we want to live by exercising life, and then we forget them, because of the narrowness, the limitation and the incomprehension of this world, so we want to reject what comes to complement our existence, as it happened between Christ and the Jews. As I understand it, even when the opposition of my spirit leads me to reject what is not of my interest, I use free will to tolerate, so I reach what I came to seek this earthly life.

Woman who Represents the Justice:--- The condition of this world, leads us to live in frequent contradictions, when we consider the struggle to the contrary, to be, or not to be what we want, and what we can achieve.

To bless God is to bless oneself, at the end he makes us un derstand that what is worth of being is not the case, but the content.

Dispossessed:-- The fact is that the poor if we are honest, we die with dignity with a clear conscience, it is the dignified death that in this world conception all yearn for and few reach...

(The conscience collapses on Mr. Gordon. Justice approaches the Dispossessed and hugs him, while the man who Represents the Sun begins to sing a song related to what happened, once the song ends, the Man who Represents the Sun advance to the proscenium on the front center side, addressing the public):--- The ignorance overloads the torment of soul; through of ignorance man gives way to selfishness, sacrifices the hope peace's, and subjugates himself to the prison of vanities.

When justice becomes effective for the poor, the world will travel on rails and the camel will penetrate the needle eye.

The Man who Represents the Sun, the Woman who Represents the justice, and the Dispossessed, leave in an embrace. Strong music, the curtain falls.

Canada August 2019.

The author of the vast and diversified experience, multifaceted of the task, which has offered us his literature and essays from the different areas of knowledge, knowing the communicational variables, now brings in his dramaturgy the alloy of fiction and reality that so satisfies the reader, while leading him to find himself as the entity of the action.

The author Literature is focusing on the human condition with all its happiness, sorrow, and day to day small victories, the author writes with sensibility and vivid expressions as he puts forth through his various writhing, the how's and whys of these different emotions.

In Theater, Stories and Scenes of a Forgotten People, anthology of short stories and theater plays are showcased, all with a powerful emphasis on those whom the author regards as "forgotten".

Contains a first part in which he gives us and anthology of stories like:

Nostalgia for the Devil, The Globe's Forgotten Ones Sealed Pact, The Sad Man of the Arrabal, and Violence at the School: these stories, in a simplified but profoundly thematic style, where those, where those lives that adapted to exist in the limitation od the worldview of their habitat, surrender to the destiny of their path, hoping to reach the grace of the divinity, from whom await justice for freedom.

The second part is composed of the: Lackey's Deceit (monologue) where a young man feels cornered and persecuted, posing a solution for salvation.

Furthermore, in The Rite of Rebellion, we will discover that intention of the liberation of those sectors of the population, that cornered in oblivion and subjected to ignorance and suffering, find not other way out than the Rebellion, so if we feel The Trial of a Corrupt and Unjust Man, we will find that Mr. Gordon, powerful landowner, uses his money to violate and abuse his Empleomania, claiming the intertervention of divine justice, after having lost hope in earthly justice.

Mariano Morillo B. Ph.D., who has been defined as the chronicler of America, seeks that the people of the world, reencounter in literature as a survival mechanism.

Publishing by: **Maple Leaf Publishing Inc.**
3rd Floor 4915 54 Street
Red Deer, Alberta T4N 2G7, Canada

https://mapleleafpublishinginc.com

To order additional copies of this book, contact:
1-(403)-356-0255

N° ISBN : **978-1-77419-015-9**

Rev. date : **12/13/2019**

Cover creation : **Marissa Flordelis**

Layout : **Marissa Flordelis**

www.ingramcontent.com/pod-product-compliance
Lightning Source LLC
Chambersburg PA
CBHW080611170426
43209CB00007B/1403